FIR
W☉RLD

Written by Steve Parker
Illustrated by Mike Lacey

1991 Henderson Publishing Limited

Henderson Publishing
Woodbridge, England

SPORT

It's a fight!

The first evidence for organized sport is wrestling, about 4,700 years ago, which was pictured on wall plaques. Wrestling was also popular in the original Olympic Games in Ancient Rome, 2,500 years ago.

Sumo wrestling, a popular Japanese sport, was first recorded in 23 BC.

Modern wrestling first appeared in France in 1860.

Put up your 'dukes'!

Boxing with special gloves was first practised in Ancient Greece 3,500 years ago.

James Corbett won the first official World Title fight, against John Sullivan in New Orleans, USA, on 7 September 1892.

Sword and bow

Fencing was an Egyptian sport over 3,000 years ago. Henry VIII founded the British version about 1540, and it is still carried out in much the same way.

Archery was a hunting skill, first recorded by prehistoric cave painters in the Middle Stone Age! It later became a battle technique. The first archery competition was probably held more than 3,000 years ago.

Home run!

Baseball is a well-known American game, but the first records of it are from about 1700, when the vicar of Maidstone, Kent objected to it being played on Sundays!

The first official baseball game was played in New Jersey, USA on 19 June 1846.

What a racquet!

Egyptian wall pictures show ball games being played 4,000 years ago. Tennis began as real or royal tennis in French monasteries about the year 1000.

King Philippe of France had a tennis court in Paris in 1308, and King James V of Scotland built one in 1539.

The first world champion of real tennis, which was played indoors, was Clerge of France, in 1740.

Outdoor or field tennis is the version we have today. It was first mentioned in a sporting magazine in 1793. The first Lawn Tennis club was founded in 1872.

Badminton, or something similar, was apparently played 4,000 years ago in China. The modern version was first played at Badminton Hall, Avon, England in 1870.

Running with the ball

Rugby, or a similar game, was played by the Romans when they occupied Britain in the first century.

William Webb Ellis, a pupil at Rugby School, England, broke the rule while playing football in 1823. He picked up the ball and ran with it — and Rugby Union was born.

Rugby League was formed by a break-away group of 21 rugby clubs in 1895.

American or "grid-iron" football began as a cross between English soccer and rugby. It was first played in Cambridge, Massachusetts, USA in 1874.

The first American football SuperBowl match was played in 1967.

It's a goal!

A kind of football was played by the Chinese over 5,000 years ago. It was called *Tsu-chu*.

Edward II banned football in London in 1314 because of the problems it caused with crowds and rowdiness in the streets.

The first modern football club was Sheffield FC, formed in 1857.

The first million-pound win on the football pools was in 1986. It went to a lucky group of people from a hospital in Devizes, Wiltshire, England.

Lost your marbles?

Marbles was played by children in Ancient Egypt, and was brought to Britain by the Romans in the first century AD.

It became an official sport in 1926, when the British Marbles Board of Control was formed.

'Owzat!'

Cricket was probably first played in 1250. By 1550 a form of cricket similar to today's was being played in Guildford, Surrey.

Canada and the USA took part in the first international cricket match in 1844. They are not so famous for their cricket teams nowadays!

The first Australian team to visit England, in 1868, was an Aborigine XI.

The first man to score 36 runs in one over — that's 6 sixes, one off each ball — in a first-class cricket match was Sir Garfield "Gary" Sobers. He did it at Swansea on 31 August 1968. The unfortunate bowler was Malcolm Nash.

Women's cricket was first played at Gosden Common, Surrey on 26 July 1745.

First past the post

Horse-riding was probably invented by the Persians 5,000 years ago.

The first recorded show-jumping competition was held in 1869 at Islington, London.

Horse racing was a Hittite sport in Turkey 3,500 years ago. The Romans also enjoyed the sport and brought it to England in 200 AD.

Polo was played by the Persians, as *pulu,* 2,500 years ago. It has also been played in Tibet and China since 250 AD.

The first polo club was founded in India in 1859. The first English match was played on Hounslow Heath in 1871.

It's a strike!

Nine-pin bowling is an ancient game first developed in Germany.

Ten-pin bowling was first played in Suffolk, England 300 years ago. They didn't have the automatic pin-putter-uppers, though!

Games similar to bowls date back 7,000 years. The first recorded English game was played in 1299.

Petanque or boules is 2,000 years old but the first official organization did not come into being until 1945, in France.

Hole in one

The Chinese claim to have invented golf, or *Ch'ui Wan,* over 2,000 years ago.

The Romans probably brought the game to Britain at about 400 AD, and it was played until it was prohibited in Scotland in 1457.

The first modern golf club, the Gentleman Golfers, was formed in 1744 in Edinburgh.

Sailing away

The first well-recorded yacht race was between Charles II and his brother James, along the Thames in 1661.

The first boardsailer or windsurfer was made by Peter Chilvers in England in 1958, when he was 12 years old.

The first boardsailing World Championships were held in 1973.

Surf's up

Surfing on canoes was a Polynesian sport first recorded by Captain James Cook in 1771.

Surfing with boards, in the manner of surfers today, was first described by James King in 1779, in Hawaii.

Snookered!

Billiards was played by King Louis XI of France in 1429.

Pool, a miniature version, became an official game in 1890.

Snooker was devised by Colonel Sir Neville Chamberlain in Jubbulpore, India in 1875.

The first World Professional Championship was played in England in 1927.

Bully off!

A scene showing something like a "bully off", the start of hockey match, is pictured in an Egyptian tomb 4,000 years old.

A form of hockey was played in Lincolnshire in 1277.

The first official hockey club was founded at Blackheath, London in 1861.

Aerobats and parachutes

The first aerobatic manoeuvre in a plane was a loop, performed by Peter Nesterov on 27 August 1913. He flew a Nieuport Type IV monoplane at Kiev in the USSR.

The first parachute jump was made from a tower at Montpellier in France, in 1783.

The first man to jump from a plane — with a parachute, that is — was Albert Berry in 1912, and the first woman was Georgina Broadwick in 1913. Both jumps happened in the USA.

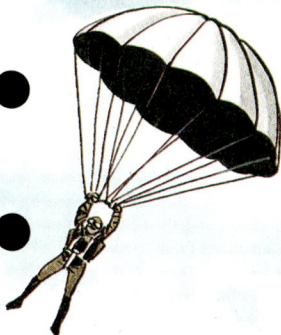

Up in the air

Gliding may have been invented by the Egyptians about 4,000 years ago. But the first recorded manned flight in a glider was by Sir George Cayley's coachman, in Yorkshire, in 1853. Sir George sent him off as a "guinea-pig". The coachman crash-landed and vowed never to fly again.

Hanging around

The first man to use a hang-glider was a monk, Eilmer. He supposedly flew from the top of Malmesbury Abbey Tower, Wiltshire 900 years ago. It was a very primitive craft, and no one followed his example.

Modern hang-gliding was pioneered by Otto Lilienthal, who completed 2,500 flights between 1891 and 1896. He died from a broken back in a crash — the first true air-crash victim.

Out in the cold

The first purpose-built sledges were probably used in Finland 8,500 years ago. Before this, Stone-Age people may have slid along on sheets of bark from trees.

The famous Cresta Run tobogganing course was opened in 1884, and the first bobsleigh race was held in Switzerland in 1889.

Skis at war

The oldest ski known was found in a Swedish peat bog, and has been radio-carbon-dated at 4,500 years old.

Skiing was used in battle by the Norwegians in the 1200s, but races were not recorded until the 1850s in, of all places, Australia! The Snowy Mountains there have plenty of snow in the winter.

Get your skates on

Ice skating originated in Scandinavia over 2,500 years ago. Bone skates were used in Britain in 1180.

The first ice-skating race was from Wisbech to Whittlesea, in East Anglia, in 1763.

The first artificial ice rink was opened at Chelsea in London, in 1876.

A form of ice hockey was first played in The Netherlands in the 16th century. Today, it is one of the roughest sports around.

Roller skates were first demonstrated in London by Jean Joseph Merlin, of Belgium, in 1790. He didn't skate very well, though, and picked up a few bruises.

Ancient Olympians

The Roman Olympic Games probably began some 3,300 years ago but there are only good records from 776 BC to 393 AD. The sports included horse-racing, gymnastics, running, weightlifting, wrestling and field and track sports of many kinds.

The first recorded foot race was in 776 BC. It was won by Coroibos, a cook from Elis.

The first recorded long-jump champion was Chionis of Sparta, in 656 BC.

Modern Olympians

The first Olympic Games of the modern era began in 1896, in Athens.

The first 100-yard dash in under 10 seconds was by John Owen in 1890. He did it in "9 and ⅘ths seconds". They didn't have stopclocks to the nearest thousandth of a second then!

The first 4-minute mile — a time under 4 minutes for the mile race — was by Roger Bannister in 1954. It took him 3 minutes 59.4 secs. The record for one mile is now more than 13 seconds faster.

The first man to clear 6 feet (exactly 1.832 metres) in the high jump was Marshall Jones Brooks, in 1876. The world record in now more than 2.4 metres.

It's been a long day

The first marathon was run in Ancient Greece, from the town of Marathon to Athens (about 42 kilometres) by Pheidippides. He brought news of the defeat of the Persians in 490 BC.

The Marathon was first run in the Modern Olympics in 1896.

Row, row, row the boat

The Egyptian King Amenhotep II is the first person known to have rowed a boat 3,400 years ago. However his servants had probably been rowing for long before this!

There were rowing boat regattas in Venice, Italy around 1300. It was the best way to get around this canal city.

A rowing race on the Thames, the Doggett's Coat and Badge, has been rowed since 1716.

The first Oxford and Cambridge Boat race was rowed on 10 June 1877. It was won by Oxford.

In the swim

The first swimming competition was recorded in 36 BC.

Swimming was made compulsory in Japanese schools in 1603.

In Britain competitive swimming began in 1791.

Matthew Webb was the first person to swim The Channel, in 1875. It took him 21 hours 45 minutes,

The first woman to swim The Channel was Gertrude Ederle of the USA in 1926.

DISCOVERY

The first explorers

Humans similar to ourselves probably evolved in Africa, more than 100,000 years ago. They spread and migrated from Africa, and so made the first discoveries of new continents.

They soon colonized Asia and Europe. Then some spread southwards to Australia perhaps as long as 60,000 years ago. Others went across the Bering Straits land-bridge from Eastern Asia to America, maybe as long as 40,000 years ago, but definitely by 12,000 years ago. They were the first Americans.

The frozen wastes

The Antarctic mainland was first sighted by Captain William Smith and Edward Bransfield of the Royal Navy, in 1820.

Rediscovering America

For thousands of years there was little contact between Europe and America, although Portuguese and English fishing vessels may have sailed to North America in the 1400s.

The Viking, Eric the Red, discovered Greenland in 982.

His son, Leif Ericson, went on to discover North America in about 1000. But his people did not settle there permanently.

Columbus and Amerigo

Christopher Columbus, an Italian explorer working for the Spanish spice trade, set out to find a western route to the Far East and India. He discovered the West Indies in 1492, South America in 1498 and Central America in 1502. He was still convinced that he had discovered the eastern coast of Asia, which is why he called the people "Indians".

America was first named after the Italian Amerigo Vespucci. He realized he had discovered a new continent when he sailed to Brazil in 1501.

The first permanent English settlers in North America were the Pilgrim Fathers, who sailed from Plymouth on the *Mayflower* and landed at Plymouth Bay, Massachusetts in 1620.

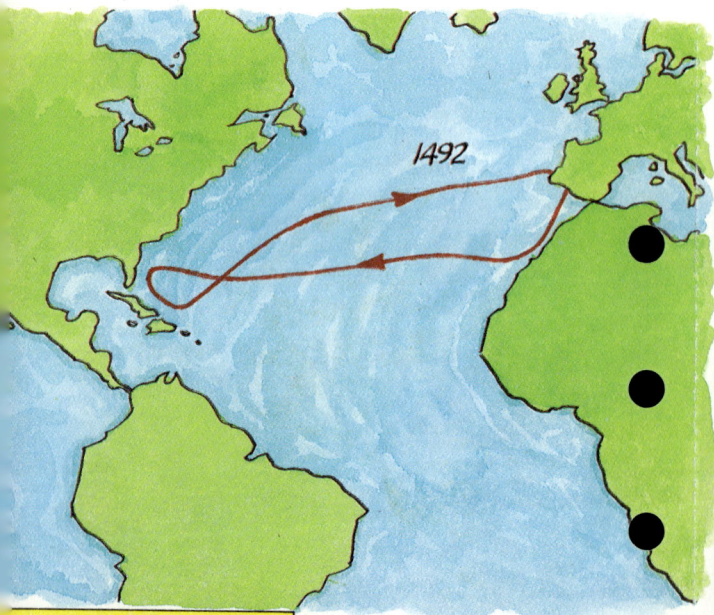

1492

The land down-under

In 1642 the Dutchman Abel Tasman was the first European to visit Tasmania and Australia.

Captain James Cook of the British Royal Navy visited the Pacific Islands and New Zealand in 1768, on an astronomy expedition. He sailed on to rediscover Australia in 1770.

The first British colony was set up in Australia in Botany Bay, in 1788, by Captain Arthur Phillip.

Planets and orbits

Planets do not go in circles round the Sun, but in ellipses. These elliptical orbits were first described by Johannes Kepler in 1609.

Uranus was first discovered in 1781 by Sir William Herschel, using a telescope in his back garden.

Pluto was first seen by Clyde William Tombaugh in 1930. Its moon, Charon, was only discovered in 1978.

The first asteroid, or "minor planet", was discovered by Piazzi in Sicily, 1801. It is the largest of the 45,000 asteroids that orbit between Mars and Jupiter, and he called it Ceres.

Jupiter

Saturn

Uranus Neptune

Pluto

The first second

Scientists think the Universe may be 15,000 million years old. This would be when time, as we know it, first began.

The Solar System

Aristarchus, a Greek astronomer, first suggested that the Earth revolves around the Sun, in third century BC.

In 1543 Nicolaus Copernicus defied the teachings of the Church, and was the first modern astronomer to make the same proposal.

Sputnik II

First in space

The first man-made object to stay in space was *Sputnik I,* a Russian satellite launched in 1957.

Sputnik II was launched one month later and contained the first animal in space, Laika. She was a small dog, and spent a week in orbit. But there was no way to bring her back.

Space, the final frontier

The nearest star to us (other than our own Sun) is Alpha Centuri, 4.22 light years (24.8 million million miles) away. It was first observed by Nicolas da Lacaille in 1752.

Stars give off many kinds of waves besides light rays. The first radio waves coming in from space were detected by Karl Jansky (1905-1950) of New Jersey, USA. His discovery founded radio-astronomy.

The Big Bang theory of the formation of the Universe was first put forward by Georges Lemaitre in 1927. The Steady State theory was proposed by Fred Hoyle in 1948.

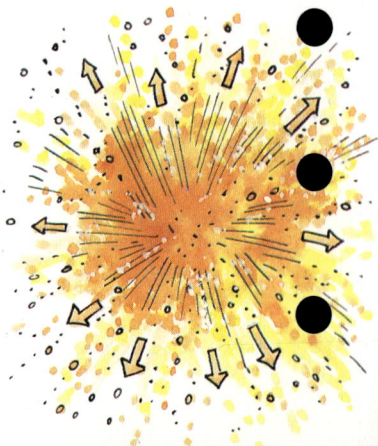

Man in space

The first satellite containing a man was launched in 1961 by the USSR. The pilot, or cosmonaut, was Yuri Gagarin. He orbited the Earth once and returned safely after 108 minutes.

Woman in space

Valentina Tereshkova of the USSR was the first woman astronaut. She orbited the Earth 48 times and spent 2 days in space.

The first British person in space was Helen Charman. She was aboard a Soyuz spaceship launched from the USSR on 18 May 1991.

Walks in space

In 1965 Aleksey Leonov was the first man to "walk" in space. More accurately, he floated around outside his spacecraft. He was tied to it by a strong line!

The American Bruce McCandless was the first person to work in space untied to his craft. He used a small rocket-jet MMU (Manned Manoeuvering Unit) in 1984.

First on the Moon

The first man on the Moon was Neil Armstrong, who stepped down from his Lunar Module *Eagle* on the Apollo XI mission, on 21 July 1969.

He stepped into the Sea of Tranquility at 2.56 am, closely followed by his co-astronaut and second on the Moon, Edwin Aldren. They returned to Earth safely.

The first wheeled vehicle on the moon was the Soviet Lunakhod 1. It landed in 1970 and wandered for 11 months under remote control from Earth.

Here it comes again

Edmund Halley (1656-1742) was the first person to calculate the return of a comet.

Halley's comet proved him right 16 years after his death. The comet was first recorded in 467 BC. It returns every 76 years. It last visited us in 1986, and is due back in about 2062.

On its last visit, the comet was met by the space probe Giotto, which flew to within 600 kilometres of its centre. This is the first man-made object to fly near a body from outside the Solar System.

Stone Age

The first inventions we know of were cutting tools chipped from rocks, 2.5 million years old. They were found in Ethiopia in 1976.

Humans may have used tools before this, but they could have been of wood or horn, which is less likely to preserve.

Heavy metal

Among the first people to use metal were the carvers of natural lumps of gold and silver, 7,000 years ago. Then they discovered that pure metals could be extracted from ores by heating, and forged or cast into shapes.

Copper was discovered 5,500 years ago and first used by the Egyptians.

Bronze, a mixture of copper and tin, was first made about 5,000 years ago.

The Iron Age began about 3,000 years ago.

People and pots

People were probably heating clay 25,000 years ago in Europe. But the first purpose-made pots were not until nearly 20,000 years later, in Turkey.

Glass beads were made by the Egyptians 6,000 years ago. The Phoenicians were the first people to "blow" molten glass into jars and other shapes, in 50 BC.

Food has been kept in wooden, clay or glass containers for thousands of years. In 1811 the first tin cans were manufactured in England by Donkin and Hall. Easy-to-use can-openers, however, were not invented until 1855!

Times past and present

Time measurement began when people started to record the lunar months, as shown by the phases of the Moon, as early as 10,000 years ago.

The Egyptians were first to measure a year as 365 days, and their calendar began in 4241 BC. They also invented the sundial to measure the passing hours of daylight.

Time-keeping devices such as a burning candle or dripping water were used until the first mechanical clock was made in China by I Hsing and Liang Lingtsan, in 725 AD.

The first watch, or portable timepiece, was made in Bavaria by Peter Henlein in 1504. It was not as lightweight as today's digital versions — it was made of iron!

The plastic revolution

The first plastic was made from plant material in 1862, and called Parkesine.

The first competely synthetic (man-made) plastic was Bakelite, made in 1909.

Nylon, an artificial fibre intended to be like silk, was invented in 1934 by Wallace Carothers.

Keeping in touch

The Sumerians were the first writers, 7,000 years ago. Their small pictographs or "picture-writing" developed into symbols that represented sounds 5,000 years ago.

The first writing using a type of alphabet was in Syria 3,500 years ago.

Money and measuring

The first traders swapped rare and exotic stones for goods in Europe, 30,000 years ago.

25,000 years later in Mesopotamia, people were using weighed amounts of silver as payment.

The Sumerians had tokens representing quantities of goods, 5,000 years ago.

The first known coins, each with its own value, were made in Turkey 2,700 years ago.

The Egyptians invented weights and measures as aids to their farming and building. They invented weighing scales 5,500 years ago.

Wheels turning

The wheel was probably invented in Mesopotamia (now Iraq) 5,000 years ago. Its first use was as a potter's wheel for making clay pots.

Carts with solid wheels then appeared. The first lightweight spoked wheels were invented a thousand years later, and smooth-running bearings 2,000 years ago.

Down on the farm

The first animal to be domesticated was probably the dog, about 12,000 years ago in Iraq.

The first farms appeared over the next 3,000 years. Goats and sheep became the first farm animals, and wheat and barley were probably the first crops.

The plough was invented 4,000 years ago.

The oldest known wine jar, 5,500 years of age, was reported in 1991 in Iran.

Pen . . .

The Egyptians scratched pictures onto stones, bones and clay tablets 7,000 years ago.

Ink was invented 3,300 years ago and applied with reed pens.

The first modern pencils, with "leads" made from graphite and clay, were made in the 1790s, in France and England.

Fountain pens, with metal nibs and their own ink rather than dipping in a pot, were first made by Lewis Waterman in the USA in 1884.

The first ballpoint pen was designed to write on rough surfaces like stone. It was developed by John Loud in the USA in 1888.

The first ballpoint pen to write well on paper was invented by — yes, Mr Biro! He was Lazlo Biro from Hungary, and his pens became popular in the 1940s.

The first felt-tip pens came from Japan in 1964.

. . . and paper

The Egyptians made sheets of "paper" from flattened papyrus reeds.

Paper like we use today was first produced by T'sai Lun in China in 105 AD, from a mixture of cloth, wood and straw.

The oldest copies of parts of the Bible are the Dead Sea Scrolls, written on a leather-paper 2,200 years ago.

The printed word

The oldest surviving printed work, as opposed to one made individually by writing and drawing, is the Dharani Scroll. It was produced by wooden printing blocks nearly 1,300 years ago in China.

The Gutenberg Bible, one of the first mechanically printed books, was made in Germany in about 1454. Only 21 copies survive today.

William Caxton set up the the first printing press in England in 1476.

From a distance

The first long-distance communications were probably by bonfires lit on high points such as hilltops. But the message was very simple: "Yes" (or "no"), and it could not be sent in fog or rain.

In 1793 Frenchman Claude Cappe devised a telegraph machine which consisted of moving arms that signalled numbers and letters on top of a tower.

Electric telegraphs, which sent electrical signals along a wire, were invented at the beginning of the 19th century. The first practical version made by William Cooke and Charles Wheatstone was used on English railways in 1837.

Give them a ring

Scottish-born American inventor Alexander Graham Bell developed the telephone while working on devices to help the deaf.

The first words spoken on the telephone were: "Mr Watson, come here, I want you". This was Bell talking over an experimental telephone to his assistant in the next room. He had spilt a bottle of acid and needed the assistant's help.

Bell first demonstrated the telephone at a lecture in Salem, Massechusetts, USA in 1877.

In 1892 Bell made the first call on a long-distance public telephone network, from New York to Chicago.

Over the waves

The first radio transmission was carried out by Dr Mahlon Loomis in Virginia, USA on 21 July 1864. It had a limited range.

Gugielmo Marconi of Bologna, Italy, used the principle to design a "wireless" telegraph machine in 1894.

Marconi was the first to make a Trans-Atlantic radio call. The experimental message was sent from Cornwall, England to St John's, Newfoundland, in 1901.

The first advertised public radio broadcast was on 24 December 1906, by Professor Reginald Fressenden from Massachusetts, USA. It played music composed by Handel.

The first British public radio broadcasts began in the 1920s, and people listened on "cat's whisker" receiver sets.

In the 1960s the first transistor radios were made in Japan. People were amazed that a box small enough to fit in the hand could contain the loudspeaker, batteries, and all the radio circuits.

The small screen

Different parts of what we call the television set were invented by different people, at the end of the 19th century.

The parts were first brought together by Scotsman John Logie Baird in 1924. He transmitted an image of the Maltese Cross just 3 metres "without wires", in Hastings, Sussex, England.

The first face on television was that of William Taynton, a 15-year-old boy. Baird paid him 2 shillings and 6 pence (12.5 pence today), in 1925.

Baird started the first broadcasting service in 1929 and sold television sets at £26.25p.

The first proper public television broadcasts started at Alexandra Palace, London in 1936.

Colour televisions were invented in 1953.

The big screen

The first motion pictures, or "movies", were taken by Louis Le Prince in about 1885, in New York. The dim film was shown at the Institute for the Deaf.

George Eastman first used Celluloid film in 1889.

The first public showing of a movie projected onto a screen was by the Lumiere brothers in Paris in 1895, called *La Sortie de Ouvriese de l'Usine Lumiere.*

Later in the same year the first purpose-built cinema was erected in Georgia, USA.

Colour movies were invented in 1932.

The first talkie

The first words spoken in a movie were by Al Jolson in *The Jazz Singer*, in 1927. Among his lines was "Hold on, you ain't heard nothing yet." The audiences were astonished, and this first "talkie" marked the end of the era of silent films.

Top of the pops

The first gramophone was demonstrated by American inventor Thomas Edison in December 1877. It consisted of a mouthpiece connected to a stylus that scratched paper revolving on a cylinder.

The first disc, and machine to play it, were made by Emile Berliner in 1888.

Magnetic recording (onto piano wire) was invented by Vlademar Poulsen in 1898.

The first tape recordings were developed in the 1930s.

How do you set the timer?

Video recorders were first experimented with in 1951. In 1956 the first practical version was in use by the Ampex Corporation for recording TV shows.

The first VHS-format machines similar to those used in homes today were made by Japanese company JVC in 1972. VHS stands for Video Home System.

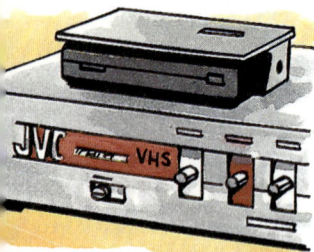

Motoring on

The internal combustion engine was invented by Etienne Lenoir in 1860.

The earliest petrol car was made in 1885 by Karl Benz. The next year he and Gottlieb Daimler built an improved version, the first practical car.

The first mass-produced car was the Model T Ford. 15 million were built between 1908 and 1927.

The power of wind and water

The Romans used waterwheels to provide the power to grind corn 2,000 years ago.

The first windmills were used by the Persians, in what is now Iran, in the 7th century, also for grinding corn.

All steamed up

The Greeks discovered the power of steam 2,000 years ago.

However steam was not put to practical use until 1698, when English engineer Thomas Savery built an engine to pump water out of mines.

The first practical steam locomotive was built by Cornishman Richard Trevithick in 1802.

The first railways

The first regular steam-railway service was between Stockton and Darlington, Northern England, in 1825. George Stephenson built the locomotive, *Locomotion.* The line was 32 kilometres long.

A few years later Stephenson built a much improved locomotive, the *Rocket.* In time trials for the Liverpool and Manchester Railways in 1829, it was the first machine to travel a long distance faster than a horse! Its maximum speed was 47 kilometres per hour (29 mph).

The first regular American railroad service was on the South Carolina Railroad. It began on Christmas Day 1830.

A bright spark

Electricity was discovered by Thales over 2,000 years ago, in Greece. He rubbed amber with a cloth and produced sparks.

Italian Alessandro Volta invented the first battery, a pile of zinc and silver discs separated by pads soaked in acid, in 1800.

English scientist Michael Faraday discovered how to generate electricity in 1831.

In the 1920s the first household items, such as hair dryers, food mixers and kettles, were adapted to work by electricity.

The first vacuum cleaner was invented by — yes, William Hoover, in 1908 in the USA.

Volta

Powerful stations

The first large-scale electricity generating plant, or power station, was built in New York in 1882.

The first nuclear power station was opened in England in 1956.

The first tidal power station was built across the river Rance in Brittany, France, and opened in 1966. It produces 544 million kilowatt-hours of electricity per year.

Rocket power

The Chinese were the first recorded people to fire rockets, in about 1040. They were powered by gunpowder and used for war.

Dr Robert Goddard first flew a liquid-fuelled rocket of the type used today. In 1926 it went 56 metres, with a greatest height of 12.5 metres, in Massachusetts, USA.

Light the fire

The first good evidence for people using fire is at prehistoric caves in Choukoutien, China, 400,000 years ago. It was made by the type of humans which preceded us, *Homo erectus*.

Lamps that burnt animal oil were invented perhaps 20,000 years ago. Lamps with wicks were first developed 3,000 years ago, and the first candles were made 2,000 years ago.

Matches were invented in 1827 by John Walker, a British chemist. They were called "lucifers".

Gas lamps were first used in the 19th century, and electric bulbs were developed by Thomas Edison and Joseph Swan, among others. They were first mass-produced in the 1880s.

The first city to have electric street lighting was New York, in 1882.

Bending light

Roger Bacon (1214-92) first used lenses to make a telescope, although early Arabian scientists are thought to have understood the principle.

Could we do without?

Scissors, invented about 3,000 years ago in several different places around the world.

The zip, or "hookless fastener", invented by the American Whitcomb Judson, in 1891.

The lift or elevator, developed in its modern form with a safety brake by Elisha Otis in the USA, in 1852.

The lock-stitch sewing machine, the type we use today, patented by American Elias Howe in 1846.

SCIENCE

Alchemists

In Greece and China, 2,500 years ago, people started trying to make precious substances like gold out of common things they had around them.

No one has ever made gold out of "base metals" like lead, but they did discover many important and useful substances — one of the first being pure alcohol!

Chemistry, mixing and changing matter, was practiced in Alexandria in 400 AD.

In about 900 Ar-razi put forward the first classification of chemical substances.

The Periodic Table which lists all the chemical elements, in order of their atomic weights, was first published in 1869 by Russian physicist Dmitri Mendeleev.

Elements

The Greeks believed that matter was made of four elements: air, fire, water and earth, held together by forces of attraction or repulsion.

Democritus had the idea that matter was made of minute particles called atoms in 470 BC.

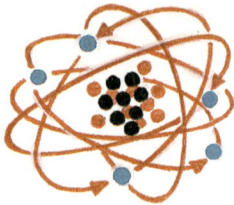

Atoms

Atoms were thought to be indivisible until English scientist JJ Thompson first showed by experiments in 1897, that they were made of even smaller particles. These are now called electrons, protons and neutrons.

In 1919 Ernest Rutherford reported the first experiments that "split the atom".

Now scientists think that the smallest and most fundamental "elementary particles" are quarks. This theory began in 1963.

Electrons

The static electricity that the Greeks discovered was believed to be a fluid that flowed from one object to another.

American Benjamin Franklin discovered that lightning was electricity in 1752 by getting it to strike a kite he was flying. He was very lucky to survive!

In 1891 George Stoney suggested that electricity was caused by the flow of charged particles he called electrons.

He was proved right in 1897 by JJ Thompson.

Light

Francesco Grimaldi discovered that light travelled in waves in 1618, but no one took any notice until Thomas Young re-discovered the phenomenon in 1803.

Isaac Newton believed light was made of particles in 1704.

Albert Einstein was the first to solve the problem when, in 1905, he showed that light could be explained as packages of energy, called photons.

Modern scientists view light as travelling in waves or particles.

Lighting up the Moon

The first laser beam was developed by Theodore Harold Maimen in 1960, in the USA. Laser stands for Light Amplification by Stimulated Emission of Radiation.

The first light shone from Earth to another heavenly body was a laser beam reflected off the Moon, on 9 May 1962. The laser was shone through a telescope from Massachusetts, USA.

Medicine

The first surgical operations were performed by Stone Age people as long as 100,000 years ago. Trephination, cutting a hole in the skull, was probably carried out to relieve the patient of evil spirits. Some of the patients even recovered!

Herbal remedies have probably been used for an even longer period.

Acupuncture was invented by the Chinese 5,000 years ago and is still used today.

Looking inside the body

Andreas Vesalius drew and wrote the first accurate anatomy book about the insides of the human body, in 1543 at the University of Padua, Italy.

The circulation of the blood was first described by English physician William Harvey in 1628.

Frenchman Louis Pasteur discovered that microbes such as bacteria were the cause of many diseases, and he developed the modern form of immunization in 1879.

The surgeon's knife

The Romans used operations to cure hernias, goitre, bladder stones and cataracts.

Julius Caesar was supposed to be the first person born by a Caesarian section operation.

The first recorded successful appendectomy (appendix removal) was carried out in 1736 by Claudius Amyand, King George II's surgeon.

Organ transplants

The first kidney transplant was in 1950, performed by RH Lawler in the USA.

The first human heart transplant was by a team led by Professor Christiaan Barnard in Cape Town, South Africa, in 1967. Patient Louis Washkansky lived for another 18 days.

The first permanent artificial heart was given to dentist Barney Clark in Salt Lake City, USA by Dr William De Vries, in 1982. The heart was a Jarvik 7 plastic-and-aluminium model, powered by compressed air. Clark lived for another 112 days.

This won't hurt

The earliest general anaesthetic was used in 1842 by Dr Crawford Williamson Long, on James Venable, to remove a growth from his neck, in Georgia, USA.

The first amputation performed under anaesthetic in Britain was by Dr William Scott and Dr James McLauchlan, in 1846.

Moving on

Greek philosopher Aristotle was the first to suggest that things did not move unless pushed, around 360 BC.

In the 6th century Johannas Philoponus suggested that once in motion things would keep going until something stopped them.

Isaac Newton proposed his three Laws of Motion in 1687. He had watched an apple falling when a young man and come upon the idea of gravity.

Magnets

Lodestone, a naturally magnetic rock, was first used by Wang Ch'ung in 83 AD for "divining".

Magnetism was first described in Europe in 1269 by Petrus de Maricourt.

The first scientific work based on experiments with magnets was published in 1600, by William Gilbert. It stated that the Earth was a giant magnet.

Reflections

Mirrors that reflect light, made from polished metal, were used by Egyptian ladies.

The Chinese understood the principle of refraction, the bending of light rays by transparent substances such as glass and water, in the 10th century.

The first eyeglasses or spectacles appeared in Europe in the 13th century.

Magnification

Lenses were first used to view distant objects in 1608 by Hans Lippershey in Holland.

The first practical telescope for looking at the stars was developed by Italian scientist Galileo in about 1609. It magnified about 30 times.

A Dutch draper, Antoni van Leeuwenhoek, was the first to make detailed studies through a microscope. He saw tiny animals and plants in pond water in the 1650s.

Cameras

Arab astronomers projected the image of the Sun onto a screen in the 9th century.

The camera obscura was used in the 16th century for drawing views projected onto a screen. It works like a pinhole camera.

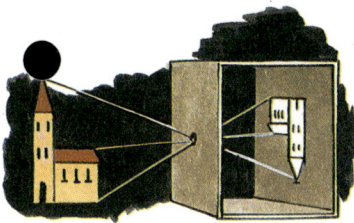

Photographs

The first permanent visual record — a photograph — was made in 1827 when Joseph Nicephore Niepce coated a metal plate with light-sensitive bitchumen.

The first English photograph was taken by William Fox Talbot in 1835, of the windows of Laycock Abbey in Wiltshire.

George Eastman developed the first lightweight camera to use film in a roll, in 1888.

Doctor, doctor

The first doctor that we know of was Imhotep, an Egyptian who lived in 2950 BC.

The Egyptians used mouldy bread, which we now know contains the antibiotic drug penicillin, to heal wounds. They also used poppy juice, which contains the painkiller morphine, to relieve pain. They knew how to set broken bones and that the pulse indicated how well the heart was beating.

The "father of medicine" was Hippocrates, who lived in Greece around 400 BC.

Hipprocates

First humans

The first humans (members of the our own group *Homo*) were *Homo habilis*, "Handy man". They were the first beings to make tools by chipping one stone against another, 2.5 million years ago.

They may also have been the first people to build shelters 1.8 million years ago.

Next in line was *Homo erectus* (oddly christened "Upright man"). They began to move away from their roots, probably in Africa, about 2 to 1 million years ago.

These people improved their skills as tool-makers and were the first to use fire.

The first modern humans *Homo sapiens* in Europe were the Cro-magnon people, more than 30,000 years ago. But by this time humans like us had already spread to other continents.

Pre - history

Ape-like creatures called *Australopithecus* were the first members of the human family to walk upright. Their footprints, the first of any two-legged human-like creature, were found at Laetoli, Tanzania, by Mary Leakey in the 1970s.

There are three rows of footprints of various sizes, the smallest ones exactly within the largest ones. This may be the first record of a family out for a walk — 3.7 million years ago.

TRAVEL

First maps

The oldest known map is made of bone and shows a tiny area of Mezhirich, USSR where it was found. It is over 12,000 years old.

Another map made of clay shows the River Euphrates flowing through Mesopotamia, Iraq, about 5,800 years ago.

Massalia

Carthage

Nile

Euphra

Traveller's tales

Marco Polo travelled to China in 1271 with his merchant father and uncle. He wrote the first travel book about the Far East, for the Europeans back home.

Travel with wheels

Wheeled wagons running on rails were used in mines as early as 1550 in England.

Richard Trevithick built his first steam locomotive to pull coal wagons in 1803.

The first railway service was from Stockton to Darlington — and back (see page 25).

The first railway station was Liverpool Road Station, Manchester, opened in 1830.

Over the land

The oldest known purpose-made "road" was discovered in England in 1970. It was a wooden walkway which crossed a bog in the Somerset Levels area, 6,000 years ago.

The people of the Middle East made the first proper roads, as opposed to worn trackways, 5,000 years ago.

The Romans were the first to build good roads all over Europe, some 2,000 years ago.

Messing about in boats

The first boats are thought to have been used by the Aborigines, when they crossed to Australia from New Guinea as long as 60,000 years ago. They possibly used double canoes.

There are rock paintings of boats in Norway, Spain and USSR, all over 10,000 years old.

The Egyptians used boats to travel along the River Nile. Boats were powered by rowers.

Down the tubes

The first underground railway in the world was the London Underground. Its first section from Faringdon Street to Edgware Road was opened on 10 January 1863. Some passengers say that the coaches have not improved since then!

The age of sail

The first sailing ships we know of were built in Mesopotamia in 5,000 BC.

The earliest ships to be steered by rudders were built by the Chinese about 2,000 years ago.

Automobile wheels

The first automobile was a steam-driven model, 70 centimetres long, built by Ferdinand Verbiest, a Belgian priest, in 1668.

Army "steam tractors" were made in Paris in 1769. They reached 3.6 kilometres per hour — a slow walking speed.

The first vehicle with an internal combustion engine was built by Isaac de Rivaz in Switzerland in 1805.

The first successful petrol-driven car or "Motorwagen" was built by Karl-Friedrich Benz (see page 24).

Over the water

The first voyage around the world was by Juan Sebastian de Elcano in a sailing ship called *Vittoria*. It left Spain on 20 September 1519 and returned 3 years later.

The first crossing of the Atlantic by a powered vessel was in 1827 by the *Curacao*, a wooden paddle boat. It took 22 days to cross from The Netherlands to the West Indies.

In 1977 Naomi James sailed from Dartmouth, England. She was the first woman to sail single-handed around the world via Cape Horn.

Steamboat

The first boat powered by an engine was a paddle steamer, which sailed up the river Saone in France in 1783. The boat was called *Pyroscaphe* and it was driven by the Marquis d'Abbans.

The first steam-turbine ship was *Turbina*, designed by Sir Charles Parsons and built in 1894 at Tyne and Wear, North-East England.

On the crest of the waves

The first designs for a hovercraft or "skirted air cushion vehicle" were by Englishman Sir Christopher Sydney Cockerall in 1954.

The first hovercraft "flew" from Cowes, Isle of White on 30 May 1959. Early hovercrafts eventually reached a speed of 68 knots (125 kilometres per hour or nearly 80 mph).

Gas bags

The first hot-air balloon was demonstrated by the Montgolfier brothers in France, in 1783.

The first powered airship flight was by Henri Giffard from Paris, in a steam-driven airship filled with coal gas. A dangerous combination that could have "gone up" at any time!

Pedal power

The first bicycle with pedals and cranks was designed by Leonardo da Vinci in about 1493.

But no bicycle was built until 1839 by Kirkpatrick Macmillan, in Scotland.

The first motorcycle with an internal combustion engine was built by Gottlieb Daimler in 1885 in Germany. Made mainly of wood, it reached a speed of 19 kilometres per hour (12 mph).

On foot

George Schilling is supposed to have walked around the world between 1897 and 1904, but his route is uncertain.

David Kunst spent from 1970 to 1974 walking around the world on a verified route.

On the buses

The first public omnibus service ran from Eastbourne to Meads in Sussex, England in 1903. It was called an omnibus because anyone could use it (*omni* means "all").

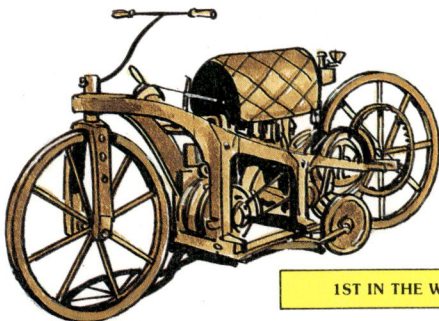

First flight

The first controlled, sustained flight by a heavier-than-air machine (as opposed to a hot-air balloon or a glider) was made by Orville Wright on 17 December 1903. He took off from the windy sand flats on the coast at Kittyhawk, North Carolina, USA.

The plane was called *Flyer 1*, designed and built by Orville and his brother Wilbur, who were bicycle engineers. It flew 35.5 metres at a height of about 3 metres, with a ground speed of 10.9 kilometres per hour (nearly 7 mph) but an air speed into the wind of nearer 48 kph (30 mph).

More flight firsts

The first plane to cross The Channel was the Bleriot XI flown by Louis Bleriot. It took him just over 36 minutes to fly from Les Baraques to Dover, in 1909.

The first supersonic flight was achieved on 14 October 1947, by Captain Charles "Chuck" Yeager of the US Air Force, in a Bell XS-1 rocket plane.

The first supersonic jetliner was the Anglo-French Concorde, which made its maiden flight in 1969.

Across the "Pond"

The first flight across the Atlantic Ocean was by Lieutenant-Commander Albert Read and his crew in a US Navy flying boat. However they stopped several times between 16 and 27 May 1919, and the total time in the air was almost 54 hours.

18 days later John Alcock and Arthur Brown flew from Newfoundland to Ireland, the first non-stop Atlantic crossing. They took 16 hours 27 minutes in a Vickers Vimy Bomber with extra fuel tanks. They crash-landed in a peat bog, but were unhurt.

Solo Atlantic crossing

In 1927 Charles Lindberg made the first non-stop solo flight over the Atlantic, from New York to Paris. His Ryan monoplane was called *Spirit of St Louis*.

Flying round the world

The first round-the-world flight was in 1924 by two US Army amphibian planes, *Chicago* and *New Orleans.* The journey from Seattle, Washington, USA and back to Seattle was 42,398 kilometres. They took six months and 57 "hops".

The first non-stop round-the-world flight was led by Captain James Gallagher from Texas, USA. He flew a Boeing B-50 Superfortress called *Lucky Lady II* and took 94 hours, refuelling in mid air four times over the 37,742 kilometres.

Polar firsts

The first travellers to reach the North Pole may have been Americans Frederick Cook in 1908 and Robert Peary in 1909. But their trips cannot be proven beyond doubt.

The first *verified* journey to the North Pole was in 1968 by Ralph Plaisted. He travelled on snowmobiles and his arrival was checked by a US aircraft.

The South Pole was first reached by a Norwegian team led by Roald Amundsen on 16 December 1911, after marching for 53 days with dog-sledges. Calculations from the journey log book showed they were within a few hundred metres of the pole itself.

The first polar circumnavigation — all the way around the world over both poles — was by Sir Ranulph Fiennes and Charles Burton. They left Greenwich, England on 17 December 1980 and arrived back on 29 August 1982, after travelling 56,325 kilometres.

Highest first

The summit of Mount Everest, the world's highest point, was first reached by Englishman Sir Edmund Hilary and Tensing Norgay, his Sherpa colleague from Nepal, on 29 May 1953.

People and Art

The oldest artistic marks made by modern humans are probably on an engraved piece of ox bone more than 100,000 years old.

Neanderthal people used the first body ornaments in Hungary, 100,000 years ago.

The first drawings were done by Stone Age people 27,000 years ago, the Cro-Magnons.

They carved human and animal shapes from rocks, bones and ivory.

The first cave paintings are 20,000 years old. The beautiful cave paintings at Lascaux, France are about 17,000 years old.

Wanna tell you a story

Human speech may have resulted from changes in the brain and voice-box, as ancestors *Homo erectus* evolved into modern humans hundreds of thousands of years ago. Story-telling probably began soon after this.

The first plays were written and performed by the Ancient Greeks. They had the first theatres and performed plays in honour of their gods, 2,500 years ago.

William Shakespeare is said by many to be the greatest playwright of all time. His first major play was *Titus Andronicus* in about 1593. His last was *The Tempest*, in 1610-11.

Making music

The first musical instruments were whistles and flutes carved from hollow bones about 25,000 years old, found in Old Stone Age sites in France. The footprints of dancers appear nearby.

The first written music was a long song engraved on clay by a romantic Assyrian, 3,800 years ago.

Read all about it

The first newspaper published in the world was *Post och Inrikes Tidningar*, in Sweden in 1645.

The earliest crossword puzzle was published in *St Nicholas* in September 1875, in New York, USA.

That's entertainment

The first international beauty contest was staged by famous showman Phineus T Barnum in the USA, in June 1855.

The first Ferris wheel or "Big Wheel" was built by George Ferris in 1893, in Chicago, USA. It was 76 metres across, weighed more than 1,000 tonnes, and carried over 2,000 worried passengers.

The first oceanarium for showing sea creatures was opened at Marineland in Florida, USA in 1938.

Cheers!

Wine was made in Turkestan about 6,000 years ago. About the same time beer appeared in Mesopotamia.

The oldest dateable wine was found and drunk by undersea explorer Jacques Cousteau. It came from a Greek ship wrecked 2,300 years ago in the Mediterranean.

Eat here or to go?

The first modern-type restaurant opened in 1725 in Madrid, although the Ancient Romans had "take away" shops where meals could be bought.

Religion

Our prehistoric ancestors carried out ceremonial burials, implying some form of religion, 60,000 years ago in Iraq.

Neanderthal people buried their dead with complex religious ceremony involving flowers and placing goat horns around the dead person, 30,000 years ago.

A shrine with a stone animal face has been found in a cave in Spain, believed to be 14,000 years old. This may be the first purpose-made worshipping place.

Zoraster of Persia was the first named prophet and he still has 250,000 followers, 3,500 years later.

Playing with numbers

The Egyptians developed a number system in 3,500 BC.

The Mesopotamians based their numbering system on 60. We still use this system 4,000 years later — on clocks. They also used fractions, square roots and algebra.

Pythagoras may well have learned his right-angled triangle theorem from the Mesopotamians, in the 5th century BC.

Calculators

The Chinese developed counting boards in 1,000 BC, but it was not until 300 AD that the abacus was invented. It is still used today for complex mathematical calculations.

The earliest calculator, over 2,000 years old and consisting of a system of gear wheels, was found in the sea near Crete.

Electrical computer

The first truly programmable computer was designed by Professor Max Newman and built by T H Flowers. Its name was *Colossus* and it contained 1,500 valves. It was really a code-breaker and ran in December 1943, to help break the German codes used in the Second World War.

The world's first stored programme computer was used at Manchester University in June 1948.

The first personal computers began to appear as kits in the mid-1970s, and ready-made in 1977.

Mechanical computer

English mathematician Charles Babbage designed a form of computer, a partly programmable machine called the Analytical Engine, in 1832. But the engineering problems were too great, and it was never built.

In 1991 an attempt to build Babbage's Analytical Engine Number 2 with new technology was made at the Science Museum, London from the original design. The successful machine was unveiled in June.

Weapons . . .

The earliest weapon, other than stones, is a broken wooden spear found in Essex, England. It is probably 200,000 years old.

People in what is now Poland used boomerangs 25,000 years ago.

The bow and arrow was invented around the Mediterranean over 20,000 years ago.

The first crossbow came from Italy in the 10th century.

Many new weapons, along with armour and huge horses to carry them, were developed for the Crusades which began in 1095.

. . . of war

In the wild, chimpanzees band together and fight members from neighbouring troops. It is probable that prehistoric people did the same.

The Assyrians were the first people known to organize themselves and make large-scale war on others, between 2000 and 612 BC. They used bows and arrows, swords, battle-axes, shields and armour.

The battle chariot was invented about 1500 BC and the Chaldeans were the first people to use cavalry as a fighting force in 1000 BC.

First World War

This war (1914-18) saw the first fighting aircraft, such as the British Sopwith Camel, a single-engined biplane first flown in 1917.

The first tank, built in 1915 by William Foster & Co, Lincoln, was known as Little Willy.

The first machine guns and the first chemical weapons were used in the First World War.

Building bridges

Arches were built by the Sumerians over ravines, 5,000 years ago.

The Egyptians built a bridge over the Nile 500 years later.

The oldest bridge still standing is across the River Meles in Turkey, and is about 2,850 years old.

Water where it's wanted

Canals 6,000 years old have been discovered in Iraq.

The first known dams are in Jordan, stone-faced earth structures 5,200 years old.

The Ancient Romans developed the first plumbing systems for fresh water, drainage and even under-floor central heating.

Pyramids and monuments

The Djoser step pyramid was 62 metres high and was built by the Egyptians 4,650 years ago at Saqqara, Egypt.

Stonehenge in England was built about 4,000 years ago. It was used by Druid-type priests for midsummer worship.

The oldest castle in the world is at Gomdan, Yemen. It was once 20 storeys high, and was built nearly 2,000 years ago.